# Professional Learning Communities at Work Plan Book

*Rebecca DuFour • Richard DuFour • Robert Eaker*

Solution Tree

| If found, please return this plan book to: |
| --- |

Name _____

School _____

Grade/subject _____

Room _____

Address _____

Telephone _____ Cell phone _____

Email _____

| Emergency Contact Information |
| --- |

Police _____

Fire _____

Doctor/School nurse _____

Principal _____

Other _____

_____

_____

# Professional Learning Communities at Work Plan Book

Since the mid-1990s, Richard DuFour, Robert Eaker, and Rebecca DuFour have championed a professional learning communities (PLC) model for school improvement. A **professional learning community** is *educators committed to working collaboratively in ongoing processes of collective inquiry and action research in order to achieve better results for the students they serve*. A PLC operates under the assumption that the key to improved learning for students is continuous, job-embedded learning for educators.

Professional learning communities are characterized by shared mission, vision, values, and goals; collaborative teams focused on learning; collective inquiry into "best practice" and "current reality"; action orientation and experimentation; commitment to continuous improvement; and a focus on results.

A PLC places its emphasis on learning for all (students and adults), building a collaborative culture, and maintaining a constant focus on results. These factors are critical to the sustained and substantive school improvement process that characterizes professional learning communities at work.

## How This Planner Is Organized

Most plan books are designed to guide the individual classroom teacher in instructional decisions. They focus on, "What will *I* teach, when will *I* teach it, and how will *I* teach it?" The *Professional Learning Communities at Work Plan Book* is unique because it not only assists the individual teacher, but also guides the collaborative team planning and processes essential to schools that operate as PLCs. Most importantly, this plan book calls upon teachers to go far beyond the traditional questions of teaching to a relentless focus on *learning*—for both students and adults.

The first section of the *Professional Learning Communities at Work Plan Book* contains an overview of the three big ideas that shape a PLC, cultural shifts that are to be expected, and keys to building high-performing collaborative teams. It also includes forms to help you work with your team more effectively as well as the standard forms you need to collect and organize information about your students and your classes.

The 40 weeks of planning pages in the second section include text and activities to inform, inspire, and challenge you and your teammates as you take the professional learning community journey.

The third section provides references and resources for further study.

# Table of Contents

# About the Authors

Since 2001, **Rebecca DuFour** has been featured in 3 video series on effective leaders and PLCs. She has co-authored 4 books and numerous articles and has consulted with educators throughout North America as they work to create PLCs in their schools and districts.

**Richard DuFour** is one of North America's leading authorities on bringing PLC concepts to life in the real world of schools. He has co-authored 8 books, more than 50 articles, and 3 video series on PLC concepts, principles, and practices.

**Robert Eaker** has been cited as one of the nation's leading experts in helping educators translate research into practice. He is the co-author of 7 books and numerous articles and has helped educators around the world implement PLC practices in their schools.

# What Is a "Professional Learning Community"?

To create a professional learning community, focus on learning rather than teaching, work collaboratively, and hold yourself accountable for results.

### By Richard DuFour

The idea of improving schools by developing *professional learning communities* is currently in vogue. People use this term to describe every imaginable combination of individuals with an interest in education—a grade-level teaching team, a school committee, a high school department, an entire school district, a state department of education, a national professional organization, and so on. In fact, the term has been used so ubiquitously that it is in danger of losing all meaning.

The professional learning community model has now reached a critical juncture, one well known to those who have witnessed the fate of other well-intentioned school reform efforts. In this all-too-familiar cycle, initial enthusiasm gives way to confusion about the fundamental concepts driving the initiative, followed by inevitable implementation problems, the conclusion that the reform has failed to bring about the desired results, abandonment of the reform, and the launch of a new search for the next promising initiative. Another reform movement has come and gone, reinforcing the conventional education wisdom that promises, "This too shall pass."

The movement to develop professional learning communities can avoid this cycle, but only if educators reflect critically on the concept's merits. What are the "big ideas" that represent the core principles of professional learning communities? How do these principles guide schools' efforts to sustain the professional learning community model until it becomes deeply embedded in the culture of the school?

## Big Idea #1: Ensuring That Students Learn

The professional learning community model flows from the assumption that the core mission of formal education is not simply to ensure that students are taught but to ensure that they learn. This simple shift—from a focus on teaching to a focus on learning—has profound implications for schools.

School mission statements that promise "learning for all" have become a cliché. But when a school staff takes that statement literally—when teachers view it as a pledge to ensure the success of each student rather than as politically correct hyperbole—profound changes begin to take place. The school staff finds itself asking, "What school characteristics and practices have been most successful in helping all students achieve at high levels? How could we adopt those characteristics and practices in our own school? What commitments would we have to make to one another to create such a school? What indicators could we monitor to assess our progress?" When the staff has built shared knowledge and found common ground on these questions, the school has a solid foundation for moving forward with its improvement initiative.

As the school moves forward, every professional in the building must engage with colleagues in the ongoing exploration of four crucial questions that drive the work of those within a professional learning community:

1. What do we want each student to learn?

2. How will we know when each student has learned it?

3. How will we respond when a student experiences difficulty in learning?

4. How will we respond when a student already knows it?

The answer to the third question separates learning communities from traditional schools.

Here is a scenario that plays out daily in traditional schools. A teacher teaches a unit to the best of his or her ability, but at the conclusion of the unit some students have not mastered the essential outcomes. On the one hand, the teacher would like to take the time to help those students. On the other hand, the teacher feels compelled to move forward to "cover" the course content. If the teacher uses instructional time to assist students who have not learned, the progress of students who have mastered the content will suffer; if the teacher pushes on with new concepts, the struggling students will fall farther behind.

What typically happens in this situation? Almost invariably, the school leaves the solution to the discretion of individual teachers, who vary widely in the ways they respond. Some teachers conclude that the struggling students should transfer to a less rigorous course or should be considered for special education. Some lower their expectations by adopting less challenging standards for subgroups of students within their classrooms. Some look for ways to assist the students before and after school. Some allow struggling students to fail.

When a school begins to function as a professional learning community, however, teachers become aware of the incongruity between their commitment to ensure learning for all students and their lack of a coordinated strategy to respond when some students do not learn. The staff addresses this discrepancy by designing strategies to ensure that struggling students receive additional time and support, no matter who their teacher is. In addition to being systematic and school-wide, the professional learning community's response to students who experience difficulty is

- *Timely.* The school quickly identifies students who need additional time and support.
- *Based on intervention rather than remediation.* The plan provides students with help as soon as they experience difficulty rather than relying on summer school, retention, and remedial courses.
- *Directive.* Instead of *inviting* students to seek additional help, the systematic plan *requires* students to devote extra time and receive additional assistance until they have mastered the necessary concepts.

The systematic, timely, and directive intervention program operating at Adlai Stevenson High School in Lincolnshire, Illinois, provides an excellent example.

Every 3 weeks, every student receives a progress report. Within the first month of school, new students discover that if they are not doing well in a class, they will receive a wide array of immediate interventions. First, the teacher, counselor, and faculty advisor each talk with the student individually to help resolve the problem. The school also notifies the student's parents about the concern. In addition, the school offers the struggling student a pass from study hall to a school tutoring center to get additional help in the course. An older student mentor, in conjunction with the struggling student's advisor, helps the student with homework during the student's daily advisory period.

Any student who continues to fall short of expectations at the end of 6 weeks despite these interventions is required, rather than invited, to attend tutoring sessions during the study hall period. Counselors begin to make weekly checks on the struggling student's progress. If tutoring fails to bring about improvement within the next 6 weeks, the student is assigned to a daily guided study hall with 10 or fewer students. The guided study hall supervisor communicates with classroom teachers to learn exactly what homework each student needs to complete and monitors the completion of that homework. Parents attend a meeting at the school at which the student, parents, counselor, and classroom teacher must sign a contract clarifying what each party will do to help the student meet the standards for the course.

Stevenson High School serves more than 4,000 students. Yet this school has found a way to monitor each student's learning on a timely basis and to ensure that every student who experiences academic difficulty will receive extra time and support for learning.

Like Stevenson, schools that are truly committed to the concept of learning for each student will stop subjecting struggling students to a haphazard education lottery. These schools will guarantee that each student receives whatever additional support he or she needs.

# Big Idea #2:
# A Culture of Collaboration

Educators who are building a professional learning community recognize that they must work together to achieve their collective purpose of learning for all. Therefore, they create structures to promote a collaborative culture.

Despite compelling evidence indicating that working collaboratively represents best practice, teachers in many schools continue to work in isolation. Even in schools that endorse the idea of collaboration, the staff's willingness to collaborate often stops at the classroom door.

Some school staffs equate the term "collaboration" with congeniality and focus on building group camaraderie. Other staffs join forces to develop consensus on operational procedures, such as how they will respond to tardiness or supervise recess. Still others organize themselves into committees to oversee different facets of the school's operation, such as discipline, technology, and social climate. Although each of these activities can serve a useful purpose, none represents the kind of professional dialogue that can transform a school into a professional learning community.

The powerful collaboration that characterizes professional learning communities is a systematic process in which teachers work together to analyze and improve their classroom practice. Teachers work in teams, engaging in an ongoing cycle of questions that promote deep team learning. This process, in turn, leads to higher levels of student achievement.

## Collaborating for School Improvement

At Boones Mill Elementary School, a K–5 school serving 400 students in rural Franklin County, Virginia, the powerful collaboration of grade-level teams drives the school improvement process. The following scenario describes what Boones Mill staff members refer to as their *teaching-learning process.*

The school's five third-grade teachers study state and national standards, the district curriculum guide, and student achievement data to identify the essential knowledge and skills that all students should learn in an upcoming language arts unit. They also ask the fourth-grade teachers what they hope students will have mastered by the time they leave third grade. On the basis of the shared knowledge generated by this joint study, the third-grade team agrees on the critical outcomes that they will make sure each student achieves during the unit.

Next, the team turns its attention to developing common formative assessments to monitor each student's mastery of the essential outcomes. Team members discuss the most authentic and valid ways to assess student mastery. They set the standard for each skill or concept that each student must achieve to be deemed proficient. They agree on the criteria by which they will judge the quality of student work, and they practice applying those criteria until they can do so consistently. Finally, they decide when they will administer the assessments.

After each teacher has examined the results of the common formative assessment for his or her students, the team analyzes how all third graders performed. Team members identify strengths and weaknesses in student learning and begin to discuss how they can build on the strengths and address the weaknesses. The entire team gains new insights into what is working and what is not, and members discuss new strategies that they can implement in their classrooms to raise student achievement.

At Boones Mill, collaborative conversations happen routinely throughout the year. Teachers use frequent formative assessments to investigate the questions, "Are students learning what they need to learn?" and "Who needs additional time and support to learn?" rather than relying solely on summative assessments that ask, "Which students learned what was intended and which students did not?"

Collaborative conversations call on team members to make public what has traditionally been private—goals, strategies, materials, pacing, questions, concerns, and results. These discussions give every teacher someone to turn to and talk to, and they are explicitly structured to improve the classroom practice of teachers—individually and collectively.

For teachers to participate in such a powerful process, the school must ensure that everyone belongs to a team that focuses on student learning. Each team must have time to meet during the workday and throughout the school year. Teams must focus their efforts on crucial questions related to learning and generate products that reflect that focus, such as lists of essential outcomes, different kinds of assessment, analyses of student achievement, and strategies for improving results. Teams must develop norms or protocols to clarify expectations regarding roles, responsibilities, and relationships among team members. Teams must adopt student achievement goals linked with school and district goals.

## Removing Barriers to Success

For meaningful collaboration to occur, a number of things must also *stop* happening. Schools must stop pretending that merely presenting teachers with state standards or district curriculum guides will guarantee that all students have access to a common curriculum. Even school districts that devote tremendous time and energy to designing the *intended* curriculum often pay little attention to the *implemented* curriculum (what teachers actually teach) and even less to the *attained* curriculum (what students learn) (Marzano, 2003). Schools must also give teachers time to analyze and discuss state and district curriculum documents.

More important, teacher conversations must quickly move beyond "What are we expected to teach?" to "How will we know when each student has learned?" In addition, faculties must stop making excuses for failing to collaborate. Few educators publicly assert that working in isolation is the best strategy for improving schools. Instead, they give reasons why it is impossible for them to work together: "We just can't find the time." "Not everyone on the staff has endorsed the idea." "We need more training in collaboration." But the number of schools that have created truly collaborative cultures proves that such barriers are not insurmountable. As Roland Barth (1991) wrote,

Are teachers and administrators willing to accept the fact that they are part of the problem? . . . God didn't create self-contained classrooms, 50-minute periods, and subjects taught in isolation. We did—because we find working alone safer than and preferable to working together. (pp. 126–127)

In the final analysis, building the collaborative culture of a professional learning community is a question of will. A group of staff members who are determined to work together will find a way.

## Big Idea #3: A Focus on Results

Professional learning communities judge their effectiveness on the basis of results. Working together to improve student achievement becomes the routine work of everyone in the school. Every teacher team participates in an ongoing process of identifying the current level of student achievement, establishing a goal to improve the current level, working together to achieve that goal, and providing periodic evidence of progress. The focus of team goals shifts. Such goals as, "We will adopt the Junior Great Books program" or, "We will create three new labs for our science course" give way to, "We will increase the percentage of students who meet the state standard in language arts from 83% to 90%" or, "We will reduce the failure rate in our course by 50%."

Schools and teachers typically suffer from the DRIP syndrome—Data Rich/Information Poor. The results-oriented professional learning community not only welcomes data but also turns data into useful and relevant information for staff. Teachers have never suffered from a lack of data. Even a teacher who works in isolation can easily establish the mean, mode, median, standard deviation, and percentage of students who demonstrate proficiency every time he or she administers a test. However, data will become a catalyst for improved teacher practice only if the teacher has a basis of comparison.

When teacher teams develop common formative assessments throughout the school year, each teacher can identify how his or her students performed on each skill compared with other students. Individual teachers can call on their team colleagues to help them reflect on areas of concern. Each teacher has access to the ideas, materials, strategies, and talents of the entire team.

Freeport Intermediate School, located 50 miles south of Houston, Texas, attributes its success to an unrelenting focus on results. Teachers work in collaborative teams for 90 minutes daily to clarify the essential outcomes of their grade levels and courses and to align those outcomes with state standards. They develop consistent instructional calendars and administer the same brief assessment to all students at the same grade level at the conclusion of each instructional unit, roughly once a week.

Each quarter, the teams administer a common cumulative exam. Each spring, the teams develop and administer practice tests for the state exam. Each year, the teams pore over the results of the state test, which are broken down to show every teacher how his or her students performed on every skill and on every test item. The teachers share their results from all of these assessments with their colleagues, and they quickly learn when a teammate has been particularly effective in teaching a certain skill. Team members consciously look for successful practice and attempt to replicate it in their own practice; they also identify areas of the curriculum that need more attention.

Freeport Intermediate has been transformed from one of the lowest-performing schools in the state to a national model for academic achievement. Principal Clara Sale-Davis believes that the crucial first step in that transformation came when the staff began to honestly confront data on student achievement and to work together to improve results rather than make excuses for them.

Of course, this focus on continual improvement and results requires educators to change traditional practices and revise prevalent assumptions. Educators must begin to embrace data as a useful indicator of progress. They must stop disregarding or excusing unfavorable data and honestly confront the sometimes-brutal facts. They must stop using averages to analyze student performance and begin to focus on the success of each student.

Educators who focus on results must also stop limiting improvement goals to factors outside the classroom, such as student discipline and staff morale, and shift their attention to goals that focus on student learning. They must stop assessing their own effectiveness on the basis of how busy they are or how many new initiatives they have launched and begin instead to ask, "Have we made progress on the goals that are most important to us?"

Educators must stop working in isolation and hoarding their ideas, materials, and strategies and begin to work together to meet the needs of all students.

## Hard Work and Commitment

Even the grandest design eventually translates into hard work. The professional learning community model is a grand design—a powerful new way of working together that profoundly affects the practices of schooling. But initiating and sustaining the concept requires hard work. It requires the school staff to focus on learning rather than teaching, work collaboratively on matters related to learning, and hold itself accountable for the kind of results that fuel continual improvement.

When educators do the hard work necessary to implement these principles, their collective ability to help all students learn will rise. If they fail to demonstrate the discipline to initiate and sustain this work, then their school is unlikely to become more effective, even if those within it claim to be a professional learning community. The rise or fall of the professional learning community concept depends not on the merits of the concept itself, but on the most important element in the improvement of any school—the commitment and persistence of the educators within it. *An earlier version of this article appeared in the May 2004 issue of* Educational Leadership, *pp. 6–11.*

---

Collaboration has helped me as an educator and improved learning for students in so many ways. Now, we each teach with our own unique style, but [our] objectives are the same. . . . In this collaboration, each teacher's strengths come out, we share those strengths, and you see that reflected in each other's classrooms.

—Amy Davenport, Social Studies Teacher, Marshall High School, Falls Church, VA

When I first came to Stevenson High School, it was clear to me that this culture was different. It wasn't just taking care of mundane tasks. We were trying to accomplish certain goals as a group. Everyone was excited about any new idea that you might have to share. Everyone was very supportive—willing to share with you, willing to work with you to help you become an integral part of each team.

—Chris Kelly, First-Year Math Teacher, Adlai Stevenson High School, Lincolnshire, IL

When we join our wills together as a teaching staff to accomplish something, we often rely on the strength of our unity to do the impossible. When we join the wills of the teaching staff, the support staff, and the parents together, we accomplish even more.

—Lisa Isselnane, First-Grade Teacher, Marjorie Veeh Elementary School, Tustin, CA

# Cultural Shifts in a PLC

## A Shift in Fundamental Purpose

| | |
|---|---|
| From a focus on teaching . . . | to a focus on learning |
| From an emphasis on what was taught . . . | to a fixation on what students learned |
| From coverage of content . . . | to demonstration of proficiency |
| From providing individual teachers with curriculum documents such as state standards and curriculum guides . . . | to engaging collaborative teams in building shared knowledge regarding essential curriculum |

## A Shift in Use of Assessments

| | |
|---|---|
| From infrequent summative assessments . . . | to frequent common formative assessments |
| From assessments to determine which students failed to learn by the deadline . . . | to assessments to identify students who need additional time and support |
| From assessments used to reward and punish students . . . | to assessments used to inform and motivate students |
| From assessing many things infrequently . . . | to assessing a few things frequently |
| From individual teacher assessments . . . | to assessments developed jointly by collaborative teams |
| From each teacher determining the criteria to be used in assessing student work . . . | to collaborative teams clarifying the criteria and ensuring inter-rater reliability when assessing student work |
| From an over-reliance on one kind of assessment . . . | to balanced assessments |
| From focusing on average scores . . . | to monitoring each students' proficiency in every essential skill |

## A Shift in the Response When Students Don't Learn

| | |
|---|---|
| From individual teachers determining the appropriate response . . . | to a systematic response that ensures support for every student |
| From fixed time and support for learning . . . | to time and support for learning as variables |
| From remediation . . . | to intervention |
| From invitational support outside of the school day . . . | to directed (that is, required) support during the school day |
| From one opportunity to demonstrate learning . . . | to multiple opportunities to demonstrate learning |

## A Shift in the Work of Teachers

| | |
|---|---|
| From isolation . . . | to collaboration |
| From each teacher clarifying what students must learn . . . | to collaborative teams building shared knowledge and understanding about essential learning |
| From each teacher assigning priority to different learning standards . . . | to collaborative teams establishing the priority of respective learning standards |
| From each teacher determining the pacing of the curriculum . . . | to collaborative teams of teachers agreeing on common pacing |
| From individual teachers attempting to discover ways to improve results . . . | to collaborative teams of teachers helping each other improve |
| From privatization of practice . . . | to open sharing of practice |
| From decisions made on the basis of individual preferences . . . | to decisions made collectively by building shared knowledge of best practice |
| From "collaboration lite" on matters unrelated to student achievement . . . | to collaboration explicitly focused on issues and questions that most impact student achievement |
| From an assumption that "these are my kids, those are your kids" . . . | to an assumption that "these are our kids" |

| A Shift in Focus | |
| --- | --- |
| From a focus on inputs . . . | to a focus on results |
| From goals related to completion of project and activities . . . | to SMART goals demanding evidence of student learning |
| From teachers gathering data from their individually constructed tests in order to assign grades . . . | to collaborative teams acquiring information from common assessments in order to (1) inform their individual and collective practice and (2) respond to students who need additional time and support |

| A Shift in Professional Development | |
| --- | --- |
| From external training (workshops and courses) . . . | to job-embedded learning |
| From the expectation that learning occurs infrequently (on the few days devoted to professional development) . . . | to an expectation that learning is ongoing and occurs as part of routine work practice |
| From presentations to entire faculties . . . | to team-based action research |
| From learning by listening . . . | to learning by doing |
| From learning individually through courses and workshops . . . | to learning collectively by working together |
| From assessing impact on the basis of teacher satisfaction ("Did you like it?") . . . | to assessing impact on the basis of evidence of improved student learning |
| From short-term exposure to multiple concepts and practices . . . | to sustained commitment to limited, focused initiatives |

# Building High-Performing Collaborative Teams

Schools that function as professional learning communities are *always* characterized by a collaborative culture. Teacher isolation is replaced with collaborative processes that are deeply embedded into the daily life of the school. Members of a PLC are not "invited" to work with colleagues: They are called upon to be contributing members of a collective effort to improve the school's capacity to help all students learn at high levels.

The driving engine of a PLC is the collaborative **team**, *on which members work* **interdependently** *to achieve a* **common goal** *for which each team member is* **mutually accountable**. All members of the faculty are assigned to at least one, but never more than two teams. Individual teachers give up a degree of personal autonomy in exchange for collective authority to answer the four critical questions of learning (see below).

## Team Structures Focused on Learning

The fundamental question in organizing teams is, "Do the people on this team have a shared responsibility for responding to the four critical questions in ways that enhance the learning of their students?" Here are some team structures that answer that question in the affirmative:

- Course-level teams that include all teachers of that course

- Grade-level teams that include all teachers of that grade

- Vertical teams that include, for example, grades K–2, grades 3–5, or French I–IV (particularly in small schools or departments)

- Similar-responsibility teams that allow resource or special education teachers, for example, to collaborate with general education teachers with whom they share students and content

- Interdisciplinary teams that allow members with an overarching curricular goal across content areas to hold regular collaborative meetings with their content colleagues

- District or regional teams that may meet in person or electronically

- Electronic teams beyond the district or region that are facilitated by web sites such as:

  - www.isightEd.com: This site was created by Apple to provide educators and professionals a forum to find each other, share ideas, and ask questions.

  - www.firstclass.com: This site has been used by thousands of organizations to create powerful online electronic communities that enable individuals and groups of people to work more effectively.

In a professional learning community, teams have the benefit of time, focus, parameters, access to information, and ongoing support as they engage in collective inquiry and action research. They work together in a continuous effort to discover best practices (in the research and in their own school and classrooms) and to expand their professional expertise to accomplish goals that they could not achieve by working alone.

## Seven Strategies for Creating Team Time

It is imperative that teachers be provided with time to meet during their contractual day. We believe it is insincere and disingenuous for any school district or any school principal to stress the importance of collaboration and then fail to provide time for collaboration. One of the ways in which organizations demonstrate their priorities is through allocation of resources, and in schools, one of the most precious resources is time.

The issue of finding time for collaboration has been addressed effectively—and often—in the professional literature and is readily available for those who are sincerely interested in exploring alternatives. Therefore, the following list is not meant to be

---

### FOUR CRITICAL QUESTIONS OF LEARNING

If we believe all kids can learn:

1. What is it we expect them to learn?

2. How will we know when they have learned it?

3. How will we respond when they do not learn?

4. How will we respond when they already know it?

In a PLC, these questions guide the conversations of the entire staff, the collaborative teams, and the day-to-day work of teachers in every classroom. You and your teammates are encouraged to reflect on your answers to these questions for each lesson you plan.

---

comprehensive but is merely intended to illustrate some of the steps schools and districts can take to create the prerequisite time for collaboration.

## 1. Common Preparation

Build the master schedule to provide daily common preparation periods for teachers of the same course or department. Each team should then designate one day each week to engage in collaborative rather than individual planning.

## 2. Parallel Scheduling

Schedule common preparation time by assigning the specialists (physical education teachers, librarians, music teachers, art teachers, instructional technologists, guidance counselors, foreign language teachers, and so on) to provide lessons to students across an entire grade level at the same time each day. The team should designate one day each week for collaborative planning. Some schools build back-to-back specials classes into the master schedule on each team's designated collaborative day, thus creating an extended block of time for the team to meet.

## 3. Adjusted Start and End Time of Contractual Day

Gain collaborative time by starting the workday early or extending the workday one day each week to gain collaborative team time. In exchange for adding time to one end of the workday, teachers are compensated by getting the time back on the other end of that day.

For example, on the first workday of each week the entire staff of Adlai Stevenson High School in Lincolnshire, Illinois, begins their workday at 7:30 a.m., rather than at their usual start time of 7:45 a.m. From 7:30 to 8:30, the entire faculty engages in collaborative team meetings. Student arrival begins at 7:40, as usual, but the start of class is delayed from the normal 8:05 until 8:30. Students are supervised by non-instructional and administrative staff in a variety of optional activities such as breakfast, library and computer research, open gym, study halls, and tutorials. To accommodate for the 25 minutes of lost instructional time, 5 minutes is trimmed from five of the eight 50-minute class periods. The school day ends at the usual 3:25 p.m., buses run their regular routes, and Stevenson teachers are free to leave at 3:30 rather than the 3:45 time stipulated in their contract.

By making these minor adjustments to the schedule on the first day of each week, the entire faculty is guaranteed an hour of collaborative planning to start each week, but neither their work day nor their work week has been extended by a single minute.

## 4. Shared Classes

Combine students from two different grade levels or courses into one class for instruction. While one teacher or team instructs the students, the other team engages in collaborative work. The teams alternate instructing and collaborating to provide equity in learning time for students and teams. Some schools coordinate shared classes to ensure that older students adopt younger students and serve as literacy buddies, tutors, and mentors.

## 5. Group Activities, Events, or Testing

Coordinate activities that require supervision rather than instructional expertise. Non-teaching staff can supervise students during videos, resource lessons, read-alouds, assemblies, and testing while teachers engage in team collaboration.

## 6. Banking Time

Over a designated period of days, extend the instructional minutes beyond the required school day. After banking the desired amount of time, end the instructional day early to allow for faculty collaboration and student enrichment.

At a middle school, for example, the traditional instructional day ends at 3:00 p.m, students board buses at 3:20, and the teacher contractual day ends at 3:30. The faculty may decide to extend the instructional day to 3:10. By teaching an extra 10 minutes for 9 days in a row, they "bank" 90 minutes. On the tenth day, instruction stops at 1:30, and the entire faculty has collaborative team time for 2 hours. The students remain on campus and are engaged in clubs, enrichment activities, and assemblies sponsored by a variety of parent and community partners and co-supervised by the school's non-teaching staff.

## 7. In-Service/Faculty Meeting Time

Schedule extended time for teams to work together on staff development days and during faculty meeting time. Rather than requiring staff to attend a traditional whole school in-service session or to sit in a faculty meeting while directives and calendar items are read to highly educated professionals, shift the focus and use of these days and meetings so members of teams have extended time to learn with and from each other.

> How are teams provided time to collaborate in your school?

# Critical Issues for Team Consideration

Team Name:_____

Team Members:_____

*Use the scale below to indicate the extent to which each of the following statements is true of your team.*

| 1 | 2 | 3 | 4 | 5 | 6 | 7 | 8 | 9 | 10 |
|---|---|---|---|---|---|---|---|---|---|
| Not True of Our Team | | | | Our Team Is Addressing | | | | | True of Our Team |

1. ___ We have identified team norms and protocols to guide us in working together.

2. ___ We have analyzed student achievement data and have established SMART goals that we are working interdependently to achieve.

3. ___ Each member of our team is clear on the essential learnings of our course in general as well as the essential learnings of each unit.

4. ___ We have aligned the essential learnings with state and district standards and the high-stakes exams required of our students.

5. ___ We have identified course content and/or topics that can be eliminated so we can devote more time to essential curriculum.

6. ___ We have agreed on how to best sequence the content of the course and have established pacing guides to help students achieve the intended essential learnings.

7. ___ We have identified the prerequisite knowledge and skills students need in order to master the essential learnings of our courses and each unit of these courses.

8. ___ We have identified strategies and created instruments to assess whether students have the prerequisite knowledge and skills.

9. ___ We have developed strategies and systems to assist students in acquiring prerequisite knowledge and skills when they are lacking in those areas.

10. ___ We have developed frequent common formative assessments that help us to determine each student's mastery of essential learnings.

11. ___ We have established the proficiency standard we want each student to achieve on each skill and concept examined with our common assessments.

12. ___ We have developed common summative assessments that help us assess the strengths and weaknesses of our program.

13. ___ We have established the proficiency standard we want each student to achieve on each skill and concept examined with our summative assessments.

14. ___ We have agreed on the criteria we will use in judging the quality of student work related to the essential learnings of our course, and we practice applying those criteria to ensure consistency.

15. ___ We have taught students the criteria we will use in judging the quality of their work and have provided them with examples.

16. ___ We evaluate our adherence to and the effectiveness of our team norms at least twice each year.

17. ___ We use the results of our common assessments to assist each other in building on strengths and addressing weaknesses as part of a process of continuous improvement designed to help students achieve at higher levels.

18. ___ We use the results of our common assessments to identify students who need additional time and support to master essential learnings, and we work within the systems and processes of the school to ensure they receive that support.

The powerful collaboration that characterizes professional learning communities is a systematic process in which teachers work together to analyze and improve their classroom practice. Teachers work in teams, engaging in an ongoing cycle of questions that promote deep team learning. This process, in turn, leads to higher levels of student achievement.

The Critical Issues for Team Consideration guide the collective inquiry and action research of each collaborative team in a professional learning community. This plan book explores these issues in greater detail at strategic intervals. You and your teammates will be challenged to "build shared knowledge"—to learn together—about each issue and ultimately generate a product as a result of your collective inquiry and action research.

Frequent, timely communication between the teams and administration is essential to the success of PLCs. How will your team communicate on a regular basis with your supervisors and administrators? The Team Feedback Sheet is one way to facilitate two-way communication.

During every team meeting, a member of the team takes responsibility for completing the form, either electronically or on hard copy. The feedback sheet and any product(s) completed at each meeting are submitted to the department chair or building administrator overseeing the work of the team. The administrators monitor the work of the teams, respond immediately to any questions or concerns listed, provide feedback on the products, and engage in ongoing two-way communication. Administrators can also attend team meetings, either at the invitation of the team or in response to evidence that a team is experiencing difficulty.

# Team Feedback Sheet

Team Name:_____

Meeting Date:_____

Team Goal(s):_____

_____

_____

_____

| Team Members Present: | Team Members Absent (List Reason): |
|---|---|
| _____ | _____ |
| _____ | _____ |
| _____ | _____ |
| _____ | _____ |
| _____ | _____ |
| _____ | _____ |
| _____ | _____ |

Topics/Meeting Outcomes:




Questions/Concerns:




Administrator:_____

Date:_____

# Student Achievement SMART Goal–Setting Worksheet

School:_____ Team Name:_____ Team Leader:_____

Team Members:_____

District Goal(s):_____

School Goal(s):_____

_____

_____

| Team SMART Goal | Strategies and Action Steps | Responsibility | Timeline | Evidence of Effectiveness |
|---|---|---|---|---|
|  |  |  |  |  |
|  |  |  |  |  |

*Professional Learning Communities at Work Plan Book* © 2006 Solution Tree • www.solution-tree.com

We encourage collaborative teams to engage in routine self-reflection regarding their effectiveness, productivity, results, and adherence to team norms. During the first few months of team meetings we advise members to begin and end every meeting with a review of their norms and to monitor and adjust personal behaviors to increase the team's effectiveness. High-performing teams in PLCs also engage in a more formal assessment at least twice each year as a way to ensure high levels of team learning and continuous improvement. The Survey on Team Norms is one way to evaluate your team's effectiveness.

# Survey on Team Norms

Team:_____ Date:_____

Use the following ratings to honestly reflect on your experiences as a member of a collaborative team:

| Strongly Disagree | Disagree | Agree | Strongly Agree |
|:---:|:---:|:---:|:---:|
| **1** | **2** | **3** | **4** |

1. ___ I know the norms and protocols established by my team.

   **Comments:** _____
   _____
   _____
   _____

2. ___ Members of my team are living up to the established norms and protocols.

   **Comments:** _____
   _____
   _____
   _____

3. ___ Our team maintains focus on the established team goal(s).

   **Comments:** _____
   _____
   _____
   _____

4. ___ Our team is making progress toward the achievement of our goal(s).

   **Comments:** _____
   _____
   _____
   _____

5. ___ The team is having a positive impact on my classroom practice.

   **Comments:** _____
   _____
   _____
   _____

# Team Information _____

## Team Contacts

| Name | Phone | E-mail |
|------|-------|--------|
| _____ | _____ | _____ |
| _____ | _____ | _____ |
| _____ | _____ | _____ |
| _____ | _____ | _____ |
| _____ | _____ | _____ |
| _____ | _____ | _____ |
| _____ | _____ | _____ |
| _____ | _____ | _____ |

## Team Meeting Times

| Day | Time | Location |
|-----|------|----------|
| _____ | _____ | _____ |
| _____ | _____ | _____ |
| _____ | _____ | _____ |
| _____ | _____ | _____ |
| _____ | _____ | _____ |
| _____ | _____ | _____ |

# Year-at-a-Glance Guide

# Class Roster

| Student Name | Guardian Name | Home Phone | Cell Phone | Work Phone | Email Address |
|---|---|---|---|---|---|
| 1. | | | | | |
| 2. | | | | | |
| 3. | | | | | |
| 4. | | | | | |
| 5. | | | | | |
| 6. | | | | | |
| 7. | | | | | |
| 8. | | | | | |
| 9. | | | | | |
| 10. | | | | | |
| 11. | | | | | |
| 12. | | | | | |
| 13. | | | | | |
| 14. | | | | | |
| 15. | | | | | |
| 16. | | | | | |
| 17. | | | | | |
| 18. | | | | | |
| 19. | | | | | |
| 20. | | | | | |
| 21. | | | | | |
| 22. | | | | | |
| 23. | | | | | |
| 24. | | | | | |
| 25. | | | | | |
| 26. | | | | | |
| 27. | | | | | |
| 28. | | | | | |
| 29. | | | | | |
| 30. | | | | | |

# Seating Charts

Draw your seating chart in pencil to allow for changes. When you arrange your students' desks, be sure to leave ample room in high-traffic or emergency exit areas.

Class _____ Period _____

Class _____ Period _____

# Substitute Teacher Information _____

## Helpful Contacts

Teacher_____ Room_____

Administrator_____ Room_____

Student assistants

_____

_____

_____

## Supplies and Information

School map / Floor plan_____

_____

School crisis response plan_____

_____

First-aid kit_____

_____

Lesson plans and materials_____

_____

Art supplies_____

_____

## Classroom Procedures

When students finish early_____

_____

_____

_____

When students are disruptive_____

_____

_____

_____

When students are well-behaved_____

_____

_____

_____

## Instructional Assistants and Student Teachers

_____

_____

_____

_____

## Special Needs Students

| Name | Support Teacher | Special Need(s)/Service | Time/Location |
|------|-----------------|-------------------------|---------------|
| | | | |
| | | | |
| | | | |
| | | | |
| | | | |
| | | | |

# Holidays and Birthdays

SEPTEMBER

OCTOBER

NOVEMBER

DECEMBER

JANUARY

FEBRUARY

MARCH

APRIL

MAY

JUNE

| | MONDAY | TUESDAY | WEDNESDAY | THURSDAY | FRIDAY |
|---|---|---|---|---|---|
| | | | | | |
| | | | | | |
| | | | | | |
| | | | | | |
| | | | | | |

*Professional Learning Communities at Work Plan Book*

# What Is Collective Inquiry?

**Collective inquiry:** *The process of building shared knowledge by clarifying the questions that a group will explore together.*

Teachers in a PLC work together collaboratively in constant, deep collective inquiry into the critical questions of the teaching and learning process, questions such as: "What is it our students must learn? What is the best way to sequence their learning? What are the most effective strategies to use in teaching this essential content? How will we know when they have learned it? How will we respond when they don't learn? What will we do when they already know it? What can we learn from each other to enhance our effectiveness?"

The focus of collective inquiry is both a search for best practice for helping all students learn at high levels and an honest assessment of the current reality regarding teaching practices and student learning. The dialogue generated from these questions is intended to result in the academic focus, collective commitments, and productive professional relationships that enhance learning for teachers and students alike.

> *A lot of our staff have become empowered where we are no longer afraid to stand up and share information with the other teachers and where we are no longer afraid to accept as being true what other teachers have to share with us. . . . At one time we would not even listen to what another teacher had to say: "They don't know what they're talking about. We're going to get a professional to come in." But now we are all professionals.*
>
> —Mary Rogers, Principal, Emmett Louis Till
> Math and Science Academy, Chicago, IL

| | | | | |
|---|---|---|---|---|
| **MONDAY** | | | | |
| **TUESDAY** | | | | |
| **WEDNESDAY** | | | | |
| **THURSDAY** | | | | |
| **FRIDAY** | | | | |

# Collaboration or Coblaboration?

**Collaboration:** *A* **systematic** *process in which people work together,* **interdependently,** *to analyze and* **impact** *professional practice in order to improve individual and collective results.*

The fact that teachers collaborate will do nothing to improve a school. The pertinent question is not, "Are we collaborating?" but rather, "What are we collaborating about?" The purpose of collaboration—to help more students achieve at higher levels—can only be accomplished if the professionals engaged in collaboration are *focused on the right things.*

What distinguishes a group from a team? Much of what passes for "collaboration" is more aptly described as "coblaboration" (Perkins, 2003). A collection of teachers does not truly become a team until they must rely on one another and need one another to accomplish a goal that none could achieve individually.

> *Our collaboration on the subject of economics was, in a word, phenomenal. Why was it successful? It was all about our attitude going into the collaboration setting. I personally realize that there are topics and concepts that I do not teach as well as other concepts throughout the curriculum. I believe that collaboration facilitates our ability to meet our shortcomings head on, instead of ducking and dodging certain parts of the curriculum because we are not comfortable with teaching it. I was skeptical at first, but now I'm a full believer in the value of collaboration.*
> —Mike Hurlbut, Social Science Teacher,
> San Clemente High School, San Clemente, CA

| MONDAY | TUESDAY | WEDNESDAY | THURSDAY | FRIDAY |
|---|---|---|---|---|
|  |  |  |  |  |
|  |  |  |  |  |
|  |  |  |  |  |
|  |  |  |  |  |
|  |  |  |  |  |

| | | |
|---|---|---|
| | | |
| | | |
| | | |
| | | |
| | | |

Week Beginning: _____

# Bradley Elementary School: Turning Over a New Leaf

The schools in Fort Leavenworth serve the military community of Fort Leavenworth, Kansas. Students residing in the Military, Federal Penitentiary, or National Cemetery reservations are eligible to attend, but the parents of most students attend the College of Staff and General Command, a 10-month course in military leadership. As a result, the school system has a 70% turnover rate in student population—an extraordinary challenge for any school looking to increase student achievement.

In 2002, Bradley Elementary implemented collaborative time for teachers at each grade level. Although many teachers struggled with this "new" idea, they used the time well, and as the year progressed, more and more teachers saw the benefits of being able to meet together and plan. By spring, Bradley students were more than ready for state assessments; over 25% scored in the exemplary range in science, math, writing, and social studies. Less than 5% scored in the unsatisfactory range.

Word spread through the district of Bradley's success. In 2003, two other elementary schools in the district had adopted 45 minutes of collaboration time, and procedures like setting norms and using team collaboration sheets were introduced to add structure to the time. Data from 2004 tests showed 68% of children scored in the exemplary range—and *no* children scored in the unsatisfactory range.

> *Bradley Elementary serves as a shining example of what is possible with PLCs. And the fact that we did it from the ground up has helped to show other teachers in our district what is possible.*
>
> —Geri Parscale,
> Professional Development Coordinator

| | | | | |
|---|---|---|---|---|
| **MONDAY** | | | | |
| **TUESDAY** | | | | |
| **WEDNESDAY** | | | | |
| **THURSDAY** | | | | |
| **FRIDAY** | | | | |

# What Are Norms?

> **Team norms**: In PLCs norms represent protocols and commitments developed by each team to guide members in working together. Norms help team members clarify expectations regarding how they will work together to achieve their shared goals.

## A Strategy for Establishing Team Norms

Ask team members to think of a past negative experience they have had serving on a team or committee and to identify a specific behavior that prevented that group from being effective: for example, whining and complaining, arriving late and leaving early, being disengaged during the meetings, and so on.

For each negative norm identified by members of your team, establish a positive commitment statement (a norm) your team should adopt that, if everyone adhered to it, would prevent the past negative experience from recurring.

## Examples of Team Norms

- *We will maintain a positive tone at our meetings.*

- *We will not complain about a problem unless we can offer a solution.*

- *We will begin and end our meetings on time and stay fully engaged throughout each meeting.*

- *We will contribute equally to the workload of this team.*

- *We will listen respectfully and consider matters from another's perspective.*

| MONDAY | | | | |
|--------|--|--|--|--|
| **TUESDAY** | | | | |
| **WEDNESDAY** | | | | |
| **THURSDAY** | | | | |
| **FRIDAY** | | | | |

# Tips for Establishing Team Norms

- Each team establishes its own norms.

- Norms are stated as commitments to act in certain ways rather than as beliefs.

- Norms are reviewed at the beginning and end of each meeting until each team member internalizes them.

- One norm should require the team to assess its effectiveness at least twice during each school year. This assessment should include a review of members' adherence to team norms and the need to add new norms.

- Less is more. A few key norms are better than a laundry list.

- Violations of norms should be addressed.

## Norms for Our Team

*In order for our meetings to be highly productive and effective, we make the following commitments to each other:*

_____

_____

_____

_____

_____

_____

_____

_____

_____

_____

| MONDAY | TUESDAY | WEDNESDAY | THURSDAY | FRIDAY |
|--------|---------|-----------|----------|--------|
|        |         |           |          |        |
|        |         |           |          |        |
|        |         |           |          |        |
|        |         |           |          |        |
|        |         |           |          |        |

# What Are SMART Goals?

> **SMART goals:** *Goals that are Strategic and Specific, Measurable, Attainable, Results-oriented, and Time-bound (O'Neill & Conzemius, 2005).*

In order to become a **team**—*a group of people working* **interdependently** *to achieve a* **common goal** *for which members are held* **mutually accountable**—you must establish a specific and measurable performance goal. The SMART acronym helps teams in PLCs establish goals linked to gains in student achievement.

## Tips for Establishing Team SMART Goals:

1. Ensure your teams' goal is aligned with the broader, overarching school-wide goal(s).

2. Clarify the level of achievement students were able to attain in the previous year (for example, *86% achieved the target proficiency score on the district reading assessment,* or *94% earned the grade of C or higher in our course*).

3. Using the Student Achievement SMART Goal–Setting Worksheet on page 12, set a SMART Goal that challenges your team to improve upon last year's performance.

> *In 2005, we achieved our SMART goal: As a district and for the first time in our history, more than 90% of all kids met state standards. And that includes everybody—no excuses. No matter if the kids are in special ed, speak English as a second language, or recently moved into our district.*
>
> —Tom Many, Superintendent, Kildeer Countryside Community Consolidated School District, Long Grove, IL

| | | | | |
|---|---|---|---|---|
| **MONDAY** | | | | |
| **TUESDAY** | | | | |
| **WEDNESDAY** | | | | |
| **THURSDAY** | | | | |
| **FRIDAY** | | | | |

# Examples of SMART Goals

A school-wide SMART goal for a high school or middle school:

> *During this school year, we will reduce the failure rate, by at least 5%, in each of our courses.*

A team's SMART goal strategically linked to this overarching school-wide goal:

> ***Our Reality:** 65% of the students in our course earned the grade of C or higher on our final, summative common exam.* ***Our Goal:** At least 72% of students currently enrolled in our course will earn the grade of C or higher on our final common exam.*

A school-wide SMART goal for an elementary school:

> *During this school year, we will increase student achievement in English/Language Arts by at least 7% as measured by performance on local, state/provincial, and national assessments.*

A team's SMART goal strategically linked to this overarching school-wide goal:

> ***Our Reality:** 75% of our students met or exceeded the proficiency target on the district/state/provincial assessment in reading.* ***Our Goal:** At least 85% of our students will meet or exceed the proficiency score on the district/state/provincial reading assessment.*

> *These goals help us to feel a sense of ownership and also a sense of achievement. You know you're finished, and you realize, yes, we accomplished what we set out to do rather than just having a good feeling about it. I think that these measurable goals make it very clear to us not only what we've accomplished, but what we still need to do.*
>
> —Linda Jamison, Retired First-Grade Teacher, Boones Mill Elementary School

| | MONDAY | TUESDAY | WEDNESDAY | THURSDAY | FRIDAY |
|---|---|---|---|---|---|
| | | | | | |
| | | | | | |

|  |  |  |
|--|--|--|
|  |  |  |
|  |  |  |
|  |  |  |
|  |  |  |
|  |  |  |

## Team Tools

Teachers can benefit from a Team Notebook to help them remain focused on the critical questions of learning. Notebooks should include:

- Copies of grade-level standards

- Pacing guides, scopes, and sequences

- Current data from the Iowa Test of Basic Skills, IRI, running records, and common assessments

- Effective teaching strategies gleaned from data and team discussions

- Minutes from meetings, including work products and grade-level and content-area curriculum maps

- Common formative assessments

- Results from common grade-level assessments (previous and current year)

- Grade-level SMART goals

- Effective lesson plans from staff members

- Team norms

With the information they need at their fingertips, teachers can collaborate on ways to continually improve learning for all.

Does your team keep a Team Notebook as one of its tools for improvement?

| MONDAY | | | | |
|--------|--|--|--|--|
| TUESDAY | | | | |
| WEDNESDAY | | | | |
| THURSDAY | | | | |
| FRIDAY | | | | |

# Wynnebrook Elementary School: Weathering the Storm

West Palm Beach, Florida, is not as glamorous as the name sounds. In fact, many of Wynnebrook Elementary School's students live in mobile homes, and the poverty rate is over 85%. Hurricanes have devastated the city, its families, and the economy—but Wynnebrook staff are not letting that stop them from ensuring learning for *all* students. Within 3 years of beginning the PLC journey, Wynnebrook:

- Raised the percentage of students at or above proficiency in reading from 55% to 81% for third graders and from 44% to 66% for fifth graders

- Raised the percentage of students at above proficiency in math from 58% to 79% for third graders and from 57% to 72% for fourth graders

> *We knew that we were having trouble closing the gap for minority students—that's 81% of our students. You've got to get everybody on the same page, and you've got to look at data. If you don't have common assessments, you don't have what you need. So we revamped the whole schedule. PLC has been the thing that changed our school, changed the climate of our school. We don't plan in isolation anymore. We just don't.*
>
> —Jeff Pegg, Principal

| | | | | |
|---|---|---|---|---|
| **MONDAY** | | | | |
| **TUESDAY** | | | | |
| **WEDNESDAY** | | | | |
| **THURSDAY** | | | | |
| **FRIDAY** | | | | |

# What Are Essential Learnings?

> **Essential learning:** The critical skills, knowledge, and dispositions each student must acquire as a result of each course, grade level, and unit of instruction. Essential learnings may also be referred to as essential outcomes or power standards.

In a PLC, each team engages in collective inquiry to ask, "What do we want each student to learn? What are the most essential learnings of our course, each subject in our grade level, and each unit of instruction?"

Ultimately, the problem of too much content and too little time forces teachers to either rush through content or to exercise judgment regarding which standards are the most significant and essential. In a PLC, this issue is not left up to each teacher to resolve individually, nor does it deteriorate into a debate between teachers regarding their opinions on what students must learn. Instead, collaborative teams of teachers work together to build shared knowledge regarding essential curriculum. They do what people do in *learning* communities: They learn together.

Ultimately, the essential learnings you and your colleagues identify must be aligned with district and state or provincial standards documents. You must, however, do more than simply adopt all of the standards and district curriculum as your essential learnings. Work with your teammates to clarify what is truly essential. Answering this critical question is a professional responsibility of *every* faculty member, a responsibility that cannot be delegated to the state, district, or textbook publisher.

| MONDAY | | | | |
|--------|--|--|--|--|
| **TUESDAY** | | | | |
| **WEDNESDAY** | | | | |
| **THURSDAY** | | | | |
| **FRIDAY** | | | | |

*Professional Learning Communities at Work Plan Book*

# Establishing Essential Learnings

Collaborative teams of teachers in PLCs always attempt to answer critical questions by first engaging in collective inquiry. They build shared knowledge by learning together. This collective examination of the same pool of information significantly increases the likelihood that members of the team will arrive at similar conclusions.

Have you and your teammates built shared knowledge on the most essential learnings for your course or grade level? If so, you are moving in the right direction on the PLC journey. If not, we recommend you begin the process by building shared knowledge on the resources that should guide your team's decision, such as:

- State, provincial, and national standards

- Recommended standards from professional organizations (such as the National Council of Teachers of Math)

- District curriculum guides

- "Wish lists" of essential learnings identified by teachers at the next grade level

- District reading and writing rubrics

- The district's standards-based report card

- Released items from high-stakes assessments

- Data from district, state, and national summative assessments

- Textbooks

- Teacher-made units of instruction from previous years

- Recommendations and standards for workplace skills and institutions of higher education

| MONDAY | | | | |
|--------|--|--|--|--|
| **TUESDAY** | | | | |
| **WEDNESDAY** | | | | |
| **THURSDAY** | | | | |
| **FRIDAY** | | | | |

# Getting Crystal Clear on "Learn What?"

A *professional* teacher is constantly working with colleagues to come to a deeper understanding of the first critical question: What do we want each student to learn?

The insights of Doug Reeves (2002) are particularly helpful in guiding teams as they address this first critical question. He offers a three-part test for teams to consider as they assess the significance of a particular standard:

1. **Does it have endurance?** Do we really expect our students to retain the knowledge and skills over time as opposed to merely learning it for a test?

2. **Does it have leverage?** Will proficiency in this standard assist the student in other areas of the curriculum and other academic disciplines?

3. **Does it develop student readiness for the next level of learning?** Is it essential for success in the next unit, course, or grade level?

Every credible school improvement model calls upon teachers to clarify what all students must know and be able to do. As teachers engage in this dialogue regarding what their students must know and be able to do as a result of this unit they are about to teach, they become more clear, more consistent, and more confident in their ability to help all students learn.

Are you and your teammates crystal clear on the answer to "Learn what?" Make a team list of the 8–10 essential learnings per semester for each course or subject area, and work interdependently with your colleagues to ensure all students learn what is most essential.

| | | | | |
|---|---|---|---|---|
| **MONDAY** | | | | |
| **TUESDAY** | | | | |
| **WEDNESDAY** | | | | |
| **THURSDAY** | | | | |
| **FRIDAY** | | | | |

# Levey Middle School: An Urban Success Story

In 2002, Levey Middle School in Southfield, Michigan, started the journey toward becoming a professional learning community. Levey is a Title I school in a suburb of Detroit with a 96% African-American student population, a 61% free and reduced lunch rate, and a reputation for having poor Michigan Education Assessment Program (MEAP) scores and for being "out of control."

> [We] worked to shift the paradigm from, "What's wrong with these kids?" to, "What can I do to help boost the achievement of our kids?" Most staff meetings were spent convincing staff members to believe that our kids can achieve at the highest levels.
> —Anthony Muhammad, Principal

This fundamental shift in school culture changed the perspective and motivation of everyone at Levey. Levey Middle School now enjoys mentoring programs, over 30 service-learning projects among students, and partnerships with higher education institutions throughout the state.

More importantly, Levey Middle School *students* enjoy success. In 4 years, Levey Middle School:

- Increased proficiency in reading from 41% to 88%

- Increased proficiency in writing from 38% to 91%

- Increased proficiency in math from 42% to 78%

- Increased proficiency in social studies from 17% to 51%

- Increased proficiency in science from 48% to 75%

Levey's school-wide motto is "Success is the only option." Their vision is to lead the state in middle-school academic performance in the near future.

| | | | | | |
|---|---|---|---|---|---|
| **MONDAY** | | | | | |
| **TUESDAY** | | | | | |
| **WEDNESDAY** | | | | | |
| **THURSDAY** | | | | | |
| **FRIDAY** | | | | | |

| | | |
|---|---|---|
| | | |
| | | |
| | | |
| | | |
| | | |

## Common Pacing

It is impossible to provide students with equal access to the same essential learning unless teachers have an understanding of and commitment to common pacing. Significant disparities in time devoted to teaching a concept results in significant disparities in students' opportunity to learn.

In PLCs members of a collaborative team work together to determine the most logical sequence in which to present the content, how much time they will spend on the initial instruction of each essential learning, and when they will stop instruction to collectively ask, "How do we know each student is learning what we're teaching?" Common pacing does not mean all teachers must teach the same concept on the same day or in the same way. It does mean that teachers have agreed to devote a certain amount of instructional time to specific content within each unit before they administer a common assessment.

### Tips for Common Pacing

- Develop common pacing guides for each unit within each course and grade level subject.

- Determine the most logical sequence to introduce the essential learnings.

- Devote more time to higher-order skills and concepts. Pacing should reflect the complexity of the concept.

- Work with the teams above and below your grade level to ensure vertical articulation and to identify any gaps or overlaps in the curriculum.

- Share your team's list of essential learnings and your common pacing guide with everyone who needs to know (administrators, teams in courses at grade levels above and below yours, resource teachers, related arts teachers, parents, and students) so that all those involved in helping students learn can operate from the same knowledge base.

| | MONDAY | TUESDAY | WEDNESDAY | THURSDAY | FRIDAY |
|---|---|---|---|---|---|
| | | | | | |

# What Is a Common Formative Assessment?

**Common formative assessment:** *An assessment created collaboratively by a team of teachers responsible for the same grade level or course and administered to all the students in that course or grade level. Common formative assessments are used frequently throughout the year to identify (1) individual students who need additional time and support for learning, (2) the teaching strategies most effective in helping students acquire the intended knowledge and skills, (3) areas in which students generally are having difficulty achieving the intended standard, and (4) improvement goals for individual teachers and the team.*

Frequent monitoring of student learning is an essential element of effective teaching, and good teachers use a variety of strategies to check for student understanding each day. However, while the ongoing assessment of students by individual teachers is a necessary condition for improved student learning, it is not sufficient. Teachers and students alike benefit from the use of team-developed common formative assessments. In fact, these assessments represent one of the most powerful strategies available to teachers for answering the second critical question of a PLC: "How will we know when each student has learned?"

> *One of the most powerful aspects of our PLC that has significantly improved my teaching is working with my team to develop common assessments. Using our common assessments to gather information shifts the focus from teaching to learning: Who is learning? What are they learning? And which strategies have made them successful?*
>
> —Chris Jones, Second-Grade Teacher, Chaparral Elementary School, Ladera Ranch, CA

| MONDAY | | | | |
|---|---|---|---|---|
| TUESDAY | | | | |
| WEDNESDAY | | | | |
| THURSDAY | | | | |
| FRIDAY | | | | |

# Assessment Resources

Just as your team collectively studied research and resources before you identified the essential learnings and developed pacing guides, your team should now build shared knowledge on "best practice" in assessment. Here are some recommended resources:

- Assessment frameworks from your district, state, or province to identify the content, rigor, and format of summative assessments your students will be required to take

- Released items from district, state, and/or provincial assessments and nationally normed tests

- Released items of different disciplines and grades from the National Assessment of Educational Progress

- Web sites on quality assessments

- Data on student performance from past indicators of student achievement

- Examples of rubrics applied to performance-based assessments

- Recommendations from assessment experts such as Rick Stiggins and Doug Reeves

- Assessments developed and used in the past by individual members of the team

- Unit tests from texbooks

Avoid the temptation to shirk this task by relying exclusively on assessments created by others. Frequent monitoring of each student's learning is an essential element of effective teaching, and no teacher should be absolved from that task or allowed to assign responsibility for it to state test makers, central office coordinators, or textbook publishers.

| | MONDAY | TUESDAY | WEDNESDAY | THURSDAY | FRIDAY |
|---|---|---|---|---|---|
| | | | | | |
| | | | | | |
| | | | | | |
| | | | | | |
| | | | | | |

# Developing Common Formative Assessments

Remember that a test is not *formative* unless (1) it is used to identify students who need additional time and support for learning, (2) students are provided with that time and support during the school day, and (3) students are given another opportunity to demonstrate their learning after the intervention.

## Tips for Developing Common Formative Assessments

- Decide upon a specific minimum number of common assessments to be used in your course or each subject area during this semester.

- Demonstrate how each item on the assessment is aligned to an essential learning of your course or grade level.

- Specify the proficiency standard for each essential learning being assessed; for example, *students must score at least 80 out of 100 possible points on each skill being assessed or at least 3 out of 5 possible points on our team's rubric.*

- Clarify the conditions for administering and scoring the test consistently in each classroom.

- Assess a few essential learnings frequently rather than assess many learnings infrequently.

> *Gone are the days when I teach my students, you teach your students. Now we teach all students and share responsibility no matter what the subject.*
> —Carolyn McMahon, Teacher,
> Oberlin Elementary School, Oberlin, LA

| | | | | |
|---|---|---|---|---|
| **MONDAY** | | | | |
| **TUESDAY** | | | | |
| **WEDNESDAY** | | | | |
| **THURSDAY** | | | | |
| **FRIDAY** | | | | |

*Professional Learning Communities at Work Plan Book*

# What Is Balanced Assessment?

*Balanced assessment:* An assessment strategy that recognizes no single assessment yields the comprehensive results necessary to inform and improve practice and foster school and system accountability. Therefore, balanced assessments utilize multiple measures of student achievement including formative assessments **for** learning and summative assessments **of** learning. Balanced assessment also refers to using different types of formative assessments based upon the knowledge and/or skills students are called upon to demonstrate. Rather than relying exclusively on one kind of assessment, schools and teams develop multiple ways for students to demonstrate proficiency.

Over time, your team should create a variety of common assessments to administer to all the students in your course or grade level following the initial period of instruction in essential learnings according to your common pacing guide.

Develop the kind of assessments that members believe will result in valid and authentic measures of the learning of their students. Your common assessments could take the form of multiple choice, true or false, fill-in-the-blank, and short-answer tests, as well as performance-based options in which your team will use the same rubric to assess student performances such as portfolios, writing prompts, projects, independent reading inventories, and oral presentations.

| | MONDAY | TUESDAY | WEDNESDAY | THURSDAY | FRIDAY |
|---|---|---|---|---|---|
| | | | | | |

# Sanger High School: Collaborating for Excellence

Sanger High School is located in Sanger, California, in the path of the city's projected growth. The only high school in its district, 62% of its students receive free or reduced-price lunch, and 18% are English learners.

Sanger's PLC journey is founded on teacher collaboration. Most departments have mapped their curriculum, aligned it to the state content standards, and developed benchmark assessments to administer every 6 weeks. Teachers analyze student scores to monitor progress and improve instruction, using best-practice teaching strategies.

> *Three years ago Sanger High School was cited as an "under-performing school." This year it was designated as a California Distinguished School and a Title I Academic Achieving High School. It is the only high school in the state selected as a Model Leadership site for its successful inclusion program.*
>
> *This dramatic turnaround was grounded in the implementation of PLC concepts in the school. Teachers committed to the success of every student began working together collaboratively and monitoring the learning of each student on an ongoing basis.*
>
> *One teacher described the change in the school's culture this way: "When we confronted low achievement in the past, we would say, 'But we are just Sanger.' Now when there is evidence of a student experiencing difficulty, our response is, 'But we are Sanger.'"*
>
> *PLC concepts are making a huge difference in our district.*
>
> —Marc Johnson, Superintendent

| MONDAY | | | | |
|--------|--|--|--|--|
| TUESDAY | | | | |
| WEDNESDAY | | | | |
| THURSDAY | | | | |
| FRIDAY | | | | |

*Professional Learning Communities at Work Plan Book*

# Using Common Rubrics

When using rubrics to assess student performance, members of your team must do the following:

- Agree on the criteria you will use to assess the quality of student work.

- Practice applying the criteria to real examples of student work until you are consistent in your scoring.

You must also, over time, be able to demonstrate that student success on your team-developed assessments is strongly correlated to student success on other indicators that the school is monitoring, such as state or provincial tests, national assessments, and grades.

> *The biggest "AH-HA" occurred in an Algebra IB collaborative meeting. We discovered that just because we were using the same assessment materials didn't mean that we all graded the assessment the same. This led to an all-day professional growth meeting of the entire math department. We came up with a common rubric that we are all using to grade assessments in each subject area.*
>
> *At the start of the day, teachers' scores differed by over 20 percentage points on scoring the same test when using their own method of grading. . . . When we used the same rubric, this went down to less than 5% difference! What a success!*
>
> *—Barbara Byers, Math Department Chairperson, San Clemente High School, San Clemente, CA*

| | MONDAY | TUESDAY | WEDNESDAY | THURSDAY | FRIDAY |
|---|---|---|---|---|---|
| | | | | | |

*Professional Learning Communities at Work Plan Book*

# Common Assessment Information

After administering your team's common assessment according to the timetable established in your common pacing guide, you will score your students' assessments in the manner agreed upon by your team. At that point, you will have data regarding your students' performance on the common assessment, but you and your teammates will need more than data before you can engage in the rich dialogue that occurs every time high-performing teams in a PLC administer a common assessment.

*Data vs. information: Data represent facts or figures that, standing alone, will not inform practice or lead to informed decisions. To transform data into information requires putting data in context, and this typically requires a basis of comparison.*

## Tips to Turn Data Into Information

- Administer group assessments according to the pacing guide (on the same day is preferred) to promote consistent testing conditions. Individual assessments (such as reading inventories) can be completed during an agreed-upon window of time established by your team.

- After common assessments have been administered, individual teachers should submit the scores for each student in their classes to the designated person responsible for compiling the results (such as the team leader, principal, or department chair). The designated person is then responsible for compiling the data and for promptly providing each member of the team with information illustrating how that teacher's students performed on each skill compared to the total group of students who took the same assessment.

| | | | | |
|---|---|---|---|---|
| **MONDAY** | | | | |
| **TUESDAY** | | | | |
| **WEDNESDAY** | | | | |
| **THURSDAY** | | | | |
| **FRIDAY** | | | | |

| | | |
|---|---|---|
| | | |
| | | |
| | | |
| | | |
| | | |

# Analyzing Information

*Results orientation: A focus on outcomes rather than on inputs or intentions. In PLCs, members are committed to achieving desired results and are hungry for evidence that their efforts are producing the intended outcomes.*

Information from common assessments makes it possible to identify program strengths—areas in which all or almost all students achieved the team's target. Pat yourselves on the back for a job well done, and recognize individual students for achievement and improvement.

Then identify at least one area of your program that could be improved. Individuals should identify problem areas in their teaching and then call upon teammates for help in addressing those areas. This process enhances the effectiveness of both the team and its individual members.

Developing and administering common formative assessments to all students in the same course or grade level is certainly more efficient than each teacher creating his or her own assessments. Team-developed common formative assessments:

- Are more efficient because teachers can divide the work among members.

- Are more equitable for students, assessing them on the same content with the same level of rigor.

- Represent the most effective strategy for determining whether the essential curriculum is being taught and, more importantly, learned.

- Help every teacher identify strengths and weaknesses in his or her teaching.

- Build a team's capacity to improve its program.

- Facilitate a systematic, collective response to students who are experiencing difficulty.

| MONDAY | | | | |
|--------|--|--|--|--|
| | | | | |
| **TUESDAY** | | | | |
| | | | | |
| **WEDNESDAY** | | | | |
| | | | | |
| **THURSDAY** | | | | |
| | | | | |
| **FRIDAY** | | | | |

# Viers Mill Elementary School: Identifying and Addressing Barriers

Viers Mill Elementary School is a Title I school in Silver Spring, Maryland. Viers Mill is home to approximately 675 students, with children from 42 countries who speak 32 different languages. About 65% of students qualify for free and reduced-price meals.

The Viers Mill transformation started when the Viers Mill School Leadership Team began studying the characteristics of a PLC. They created a core set of initiatives and strategies to address the unique challenges facing their school community:

- **A whole-school focus on reading comprehension:** Educators identified a common mission and vision. They committed to increasing the performance of all students in reading comprehension and reinforced that message at every opportunity.

- **Use of collaborative teams:** Educators used teams to determine essential outcomes, create common assessments, review student work, and create interventions for students needing extra time and support.

- **Improved communication to parents:** Individual student progress reports were sent home with students every 3 weeks. Progress reports were aligned with the district report card—and were sent in English and Spanish.

- **Creative approaches to cultural barriers:** The new Family Learning Nights program increased parent involvement and increased student and family connections to the school.

In 2005, Viers was selected as a state and a national Blue Ribbon School of Excellence.

| MONDAY | TUESDAY | WEDNESDAY | THURSDAY | FRIDAY |
|--------|---------|-----------|----------|--------|
|        |         |           |          |        |
|        |         |           |          |        |
|        |         |           |          |        |
|        |         |           |          |        |
|        |         |           |          |        |

# Using Results to Motivate

In order to promote continuous improvement, feedback must not only be timely, it must also be effective. Feedback can encourage effort and improvement, but it can and often is used in ways that create a sense of hopelessness. Whenever an activity is viewed as a competition, there will be winners and losers. When feedback to students takes the form of grades, they are likely to see assessment as a competition or a way to compare their achievements with others. There will always be a best and a worst. Instead, the goal of feedback is to provide every student with the information and support necessary to fuel continuous improvement.

## Tips for Motivating Students

- Teach students the criteria you will use to judge the quality of their work, and provide examples.

- Engage students in assessing their own work according to the criteria for quality work.

- Whenever possible, provide each student with feedback on his or her progress and strategies for improving, rather than assign a grade.

- Use the student's own previous performance as a benchmark for improvement, rather than the performance of other students in the class, district, or state.

- Use feedback on results to inform, not punish.

- Provide feedback to students and their parents in an easily interpreted, user-friendly format.

- Use a balance of summative assessment and a variety of formative assessment to give students multiple ways to demonstrate proficiency.

- Celebrate small wins.

|  | | | | |
|---|---|---|---|---|
| **MONDAY** | | | | |
| **TUESDAY** | | | | |
| **WEDNESDAY** | | | | |
| **THURSDAY** | | | | |
| **FRIDAY** | | | | |

# Marjorie Veeh Elementary School: Responding to Change

When Marjorie Veeh Elementary School was founded in 1963 in Tustin, California, most students were from white economically secure families. Today, however, the average annual family income of Veeh students is less than $15,000. Multiple families share small apartments. Over 25% of Veeh parents did not graduate from high school, and many lack English skills.

In response to its new demographics, the staff at Veeh began the arduous process of redesigning their instructional program. Literacy is the foundation of a new school vision grounded in the powerful concepts of learning for all, collaboration, and a focus on results. In 3 years, Veeh:

- Improved state standardized assessment results by 87 points. Economically disadvantaged students improved by 116 points, and Hispanic students improved by 144 points—378% better than Veeh's goal

- Increased proficiency in language arts by 43% and in mathematics by 50%

In 2004, Veeh was recognized as a California Distinguished School and a Title I Achieving School. But Veeh is not yet satisfied, because Veeh's mission is not for *most* students to become literate, or for *more* students to meet standards: At Marjorie Veeh Elementary School, *all* students will become literate and meet standards.

> *We know that our students' needs are so numerous, and their obstacles are so daunting, that the only way we can assure their success is by working together. Every individual in our school community is essential, every resource is vital, and every minute is precious. Our success comes from our genuine love for our students and our singular dedication to fulfill our mission.*
>
> —Mike Mattos, Past Principal

| MONDAY | | | | | |
|--------|--|--|--|--|--|
| **TUESDAY** | | | | | |
| **WEDNESDAY** | | | | | |
| **THURSDAY** | | | | | |
| **FRIDAY** | | | | | |

*Professional Learning Communities at Work Plan Book*

# How Will We Respond?

1. What do we want each student to learn?
2. How will we know when each student has learned it?
3. *How will we respond when a student experiences difficulty in learning?*
4. How will we respond when a student already knows it?

Imagine four students assigned to four different teachers of the same course or grade level in a traditional school. Although each student experiences difficulty in learning, the teachers in the four isolated classrooms respond in very different ways.

The first teacher concludes that the student lacks the necessary ability and recommends the student be transferred into a program with less rigorous content. The second teacher assumes the student lacks motivation and fails or retains the student to teach him or her to be more responsible. The third promotes the struggling student in the belief that retention would be a blow to his or her self-esteem or in the hope that the student will be more successful with another year of development. The fourth teacher works with the student before and after school and during lunch until the student becomes proficient.

Professional learning communities do not leave the third critical question, "How will we respond when a student does not learn?" up to each teacher to decide. Instead, they develop a systematic school-wide plan that ensures every student receives additional time and support for learning as soon as he or she experience difficulty—regardless of who the teacher might be. The intervention occurs during the school day, and students are directed rather than invited to utilize the support.

| MONDAY | TUESDAY | WEDNESDAY | THURSDAY | FRIDAY |
|--------|---------|-----------|----------|--------|
|        |         |           |          |        |
|        |         |           |          |        |
|        |         |           |          |        |
|        |         |           |          |        |
|        |         |           |          |        |

# Creating Systematic Interventions

*Systematic intervention:* A school-wide plan that ensures every student in every course or grade level will receive additional time and support for learning as soon as he or she experiences difficulty in acquiring essential knowledge and skills. In a PLC, the intervention occurs during the school day, and students are required rather than invited to devote the extra time and secure the extra support for learning. Because student learning is monitored continuously, this intervention occurs as soon as a student begins to struggle.

Have you and your teammates created systematic interventions for your course or grade level? If so, you are moving in the right direction on the PLC journey. If not, we recommend you begin by examining your current interventions by asking:

- Are our students assured EXTRA TIME AND SUPPORT for learning?

- Is our response TIMELY? How quickly are we able to identify the kids who need extra time and support? Is our focus prompt intervention rather than sluggish remediation?

- Is our response DIRECTIVE rather than invitational? Are kids invited to put in extra time or does our system ensure they put in extra time?

- Is our response SYSTEMATIC? Do kids receive this intervention according to a school-wide plan rather than at the discretion of individual teachers?

| | MONDAY | TUESDAY | WEDNESDAY | THURSDAY | FRIDAY |
|---|---|---|---|---|---|
| | | | | | |

## Tips for Interventions

- Ensure common understanding of the term "systematic intervention."

- Design a fluid system of intervention, rather than a permanent support system for individual students. Once students become proficient in the problem area, they should be weaned from the system. There should be an easy flow of students into and out of the various levels of the program of support.

- The system of intervention should be used to support the work of collaborative teams rather than individual teachers. Common curriculum, common pacing, common assessments, and common standards for grading student work are all essential to systematic interventions.

- Your intervention plan should be based upon the unique context of your school. Developing your own plan, rather than adopting another school's, will create far more ownership in and commitment to that plan.

- Realize that no support system will compensate for weak and ineffective teaching. Teachers must constantly examine their practices and expand their skills. But no matter how skillful the professional, it is likely that some students will not master the intended learning. At that point the system of interventions comes to the aid of both students and teachers.

> *I'm not just a teacher at Boone's Mill; I'm also a parent. It is very reassuring to know that if my children experience difficulty, it won't fall to a single teacher to solve the problem. At Boones Mill, an entire team of adults will rally around any child who needs extra support to be successful.*
>
> *—Lisa Doss, Third-Grade Teacher, Boones Mill Elementary School, Franklin County, VA*

| MONDAY | | | | |
|--------|--------|--------|--------|--------|
| | | | | |
| **TUESDAY** | | | | |
| | | | | |
| **WEDNESDAY** | | | | |
| | | | | |
| **THURSDAY** | | | | |
| | | | | |
| **FRIDAY** | | | | |

| | | |
|---|---|---|
| | | |
| | | |
| | | |
| | | |
| | | |

# Southmoreland Junior High: A Rural Success Story

The staff at Southmoreland Junior High School knew they could do better—and they *had* to do better, because their students had no other options. Located 40 miles from Pittsburgh, Southmoreland is the only junior high in its district. Though the area had experienced a brief period of affluence from the steel industry near the turn of the 20th century, its economic decline began even before the Depression—and never recovered. Today, the largest town in the district has just 5,000 residents.

In 2003, the state placed Southmoreland in the warning category due to the poor performance of economically disadvantaged students on standardized assessments. In the 2 years after beginning the PLC journey in 2003, Southmoreland Junior High:

- Increased proficient and advanced eighth-grade math scores from 39% to 72%

- Increased proficient and advanced eighth-grade reading scores from 55% to 77%

- Doubled the proficiency of the subgroup of economically disadvantaged students

*We have undergone great change at Southmoreland Junior High School. We attribute our collaborative culture as the significant factor in the improved performance of students. A new school schedule was adopted that built in teaming time as a regular part of the school day, and teaming time was focused on issues of improved learning. Our teams develop interventions that try to ensure student success. Best of all, we constantly evaluate our teamwork and embrace change as a means to get better. As rewarding as it is to know that teachers feel good about our collaborative culture, the proof lies with our results.*

—Timothy Scott, Principal

|  | MONDAY | TUESDAY | WEDNESDAY | THURSDAY | FRIDAY |
|---|---|---|---|---|---|
|  |  |  |  |  |  |
|  |  |  |  |  |  |
|  |  |  |  |  |  |
|  |  |  |  |  |  |
|  |  |  |  |  |  |

## Action Orientation

*Action orientation:* A predisposition to learn by doing; moving quickly to turn aspirations into actions and visions into realities.

Members of PLCs understand that the most powerful learning always occurs in a context of taking action, and they value engagement and reflective experience as the most effective teachers. The very reason that you should work together in teams and engage in collective inquiry is to serve as a catalyst for *action.* No school will experience gains in student achievement merely by writing a new vision statement or developing a strategic plan. You will not see improvement until you begin to *act* differently.

> In the traditional schools where I spent the first 11 years of my career, teachers were isolated. While they might occasionally have shared ideas and talked about what they were doing in their classrooms, there was no formalized expectation that teachers would work together to identify and amplify best practices. . . .
>
> Professional learning communities are different. Teachers agree to work together to examine and to reflect, collaborating in ways that are often foreign in our profession. The focus of teacher learning teams is on identifying what works for students. Shared knowledge is valued above all, and teachers have to be willing to open their practice to review and revision. This collaboration leads to growth and to change . . . and holds great power to reform what happens in our schools.*
>
> —Bill Ferriter, Sixth-Grade Teacher, Salem Middle School, Raleigh, NC

*Used with permission of the National Staff Development Council, www.nsdc.org, 2006. All rights reserved.

| | | | | | |
|---|---|---|---|---|---|
| **MONDAY** | | | | | |
| **TUESDAY** | | | | | |
| **WEDNESDAY** | | | | | |
| **THURSDAY** | | | | | |
| **FRIDAY** | | | | | |

# Adams Middle School: Streamlining Improvement

Adams Middle School is in Westland, Michigan, a blue-collar suburb of Detroit, with many of the characteristics of a "south end" school. Many Adams students come from single-parent homes or live with nonparental guardians. In its district, Adams has the largest population of students considered economically disadvantaged by the state of Michigan: 60% qualify for free or reduced lunch.

Adams used the process of becoming a PLC as an opportunity to consolidate all of the school improvement requirements that had come their way, including NCA School Improvement, MEAP Improvement, Title I, and MI Plan. Using the four critical questions of a PLC, Adams staff took a single, focused approach to sustained school improvement. As a result, Adams has surpassed the other middle schools in the district in student achievement. By using common pacing guides, common formative assessments, and other PLC strategies, Adams has:

- Increased proficiency in English language arts from 49.2% in 2001 to 63.3% in 2005

- Increased proficiency in science from 10.4% in 2001 to 72.4% in 2005

- Led the district in MEAP scores for English, math, science, and social studies from 2003 to 2005, with scores well above the state averages

*Adams Middle School has built a deep, meaningful collaborative culture and has transformed our school by making learning rather than teaching its fundamental purpose. The staff members take justifiable pride in the powerful results their collective efforts have produced, even as they look for additional ways to reach all students.*

—Dave Ingham, Principal

| MONDAY | | | | |
|--------|--|--|--|--|
| **TUESDAY** | | | | |
| **WEDNESDAY** | | | | |
| **THURSDAY** | | | | |
| **FRIDAY** | | | | |

# What Is a *Professional* Teacher?

Teachers represent the heartbeat of a school, and the changes essential to school improvement must be manifested by individual teachers at the classroom level. You must continue to "practice" your profession through the constant exploration of the art and science of teaching for your entire career. *Professional* teachers:

- **Emphasize learning rather than teaching.** Professional teachers ask, "What are the best instructional strategies to help all of my students learn what is intended?"

- **Emphasize active student engagement with significant content.** Professional teachers ask, "How can I engage students in real and meaningful ways over the sustained period of time that is necessary for students to reach high levels of learning?"

- **Focus on student performance and production.** Professional teachers ask, "How can the performances and products be made more authentic? What standards should students be expected to meet? Have my teammates and I agreed on the criteria we use in evaluating the quality of student work, and do we apply the criteria consistently?"

- **Routinely collaborate with colleagues.** Professional teachers ask, "How can I learn from my colleagues and contribute to their learning as we work interdependently to achieve our common goals?"

- **Become students of teaching and consumers of research.** Professional teachers ask, "What new advances in curriculum, instruction, and assessment can I implement to improve learning for all students?"

- **Function as leaders:** Professional teachers ask, "How can I be a leader in my school's journey to improve student learning?"

| | | | | |
|---|---|---|---|---|
| **MONDAY** | | | | |
| **TUESDAY** | | | | |
| **WEDNESDAY** | | | | |
| **THURSDAY** | | | | |
| **FRIDAY** | | | | |

# Centreville High School: Something Extra

Centreville High School opened in 1988 in suburban Clifton, Virginia, at the edge of the Dulles technology corridor. Centreville's growing enrollment has presented many challenges, both logistical and cultural. By 1998, the school facility was supplemented by over 30 trailer classrooms.

Centreville strives to be a center of creativity and innovation despite these challenges. Centreville began its PLC journey in 2004; by spring of 2006, it had been named one of the 100 Best Schools in America by *Newsweek*. With four computer labs and multiple wireless labs, Centreville students enjoy many opportunities to learn. More than 80% of all students engage in at least one extra- or cocurricular activity. In 2 years, Centreville:

- Increased enrollment in Honors and AP courses by 15% overall, including increases of 10–20% in minority subgroups

- Significantly decreased the number of students receiving grades of D or F

> *Through the core philosophy of collaboration and collegiality, Centreville High School's faculty and staff have made tremendous gains working with students who have traditionally met with failure. Providing extra time and support, sharing assessment practices, discussing instructional best practice, and doing whatever it takes by taking ownership for all students have transcended the bounds of what many thought was possible. We are now, through the efforts of the staff and tenets of PLC, a top-100 school in the nation.*
> —Peter Noonan, Past Principal

| | | | | |
|---|---|---|---|---|
| **MONDAY** | | | | |
| **TUESDAY** | | | | |
| **WEDNESDAY** | | | | |
| **THURSDAY** | | | | |
| **FRIDAY** | | | | |

## Kildeer Countryside Elementary School: Good to Great

In 2002, the faculty at Kildeer Countryside Elementary School in Long Grove, Illinois, were hardworking, dedicated professionals who spent hours creating elaborate lesson plans and tutoring their students before and after class. At that time the number of third- and fifth-grade students meeting or exceeding state standards in reading and math averaged 85%.

Kildeer was a good school, and the faculty shared school-wide goals. But classrooms operated independently, and teachers often made isolated, parallel efforts rather than collaborative, systematic efforts to improve student learning. They cooperated rather than collaborated. To become a great school, teachers had to start collaborating: on the critical questions on learning, on the creation of common assessments, and on school-wide, systematic interventions.

By 2006, the number of students meeting or exceeding state standards had risen to 95%. Kildeer has been recognized as one of the top 50 elementary schools in Illinois for 3 years in a row—out of 2,500 schools. What made the difference? Collaboration—and an insistence on continuous improvement, with high expectations for students and teachers alike.

> You don't find time for collaboration—you make time for collaboration. Time is precious in schools, and we don't have a secret closet or desk drawer somewhere where we hide extra time. If our school wants time for collaboration, we make time for collaboration in our daily schedule. In our school, time for collaboration is a priority.
>
> —Greg Grana, Principal

| | | | | |
|---|---|---|---|---|
| **MONDAY** | | | | |
| **TUESDAY** | | | | |
| **WEDNESDAY** | | | | |
| **THURSDAY** | | | | |
| **FRIDAY** | | | | |

*Professional Learning Communities at Work Plan Book*

# Creating Opportunity for Many Winners

Schools have always had ways to recognize individual students. It is not unusual for a school to have honor rolls, valedictorians, captains of athletic teams, or National Honor Societies. And in most schools, the overwhelming majority of students realize from the very day they enter the school that they have no chance of ever receiving that recognition.

It will be difficult to create a culture of success in a school that limits recognition of success to an elite few. When schools develop systems to honor not only the highest academic achievement, but also improvement, character, service, and persistence, virtually all students can come to believe that school can be a place where they have the chance to be recognized and celebrated.

Celebrations are a powerful form of communication that can clarify what is valued and important, can motivate individuals, and can contribute to a culture of continuous improvement. Recognize and celebrate individual students when they do the following:

- Reach a designated standard of achievement.

- Demonstrate significant improvement.

- Demonstrate the qualities you are attempting to promote, such as empathy and perseverance.

- Complete a challenging project.

- Engage in community service.

> *It's our feeling that during an entire year, every child should have a cause to celebrate either their achievement or their improvement. That's just logical.*
> —Cynthia Jones, Third- and Fourth-Grade Teacher, Cason Lane Academy, Murfreesboro, TN

| | | | | |
|---|---|---|---|---|
| **MONDAY** | | | | |
| **TUESDAY** | | | | |
| **WEDNESDAY** | | | | |
| **THURSDAY** | | | | |
| **FRIDAY** | | | | |

*Professional Learning Communities at Work Plan Book*

<table>
<tr><td></td><td></td><td></td></tr>
<tr><td></td><td></td><td></td></tr>
<tr><td></td><td></td><td></td></tr>
<tr><td></td><td></td><td></td></tr>
<tr><td></td><td></td><td></td></tr>
</table>

# Celebration: A Key to Sustaining PLCs

The single best strategy to sustain the process to implement PLC concepts is to plan for and celebrate small wins along the way. Recognizing and celebrating the effort and achievements of both students and adults is also a powerful tool for communicating what is valued in the school.

## Tips for Celebrating

- Explicitly state the purpose of celebration.

- Make celebration everyone's responsibility.

- Establish a clear link between the recognition and the behavior or commitment you are attempting to encourage or reinforce.

- Find creative, visible ways to recognize each student who meets specific academic goals.

- Recognize student curricular and noncurricular achievements in daily school announcements, in class and school newsletters, and at awards assemblies.

- Share professional learning and achievements at weekly team meetings and monthly staff meetings.

- Recognize improvement as well as achievement.

- Create opportunities to have many winners.

| MONDAY | | | | |
|--------|---|---|---|---|
| **TUESDAY** | | | | |
| **WEDNESDAY** | | | | |
| **THURSDAY** | | | | |
| **FRIDAY** | | | | |

## The Power of Storytelling

*Every aspect of the PLC is a circle that mirrors the complexity of working with people. We discovered this, or rather we stumbled upon it, while exploring the power of celebrating our success.*

*We celebrated everything. Everyone's focus is standardized tests—but why should "they" describe "us"? We got creative. Our principal asked alumni to tell us stories about teachers who impacted them. We bound those stories into notebooks and added to it every year. The heartfelt stories poured in. In fact, the stories are still coming. Those stories define us.*

*We milked every opportunity to celebrate big and small successes. We focused less on pass rates and more on participation rates. We celebrated improvement rather than just being at the top. Teachers, students, parents, and the community could not get away from hearing about our many successes. We used newspaper articles, auto dialers, the electronic marquee, stump appearances, local community events and service clubs, listservs, coffees with the principal, and web pages.*

*As we celebrated more and more, morale hit all time highs. Ninety-two percent of the teachers voted to adopt a weekly collaboration schedule that impacted contact minutes and increased their teaching day. Our parent organization increased membership by almost 300% and poured the money back into the classroom in teacher grants and gifts. A 400% increase in the amount of students taking Advanced Placement classes appeared out of nowhere.*

*The decision to celebrate everything fostered success and, in turn, created more things to celebrate. It is the perfect circle, and it was simple to do.*

—George Knights, Past Assistant Principal, San Clemente High School, San Clemente, CA

| | | | | |
|---|---|---|---|---|
| **MONDAY** | | | | |
| **TUESDAY** | | | | |
| **WEDNESDAY** | | | | |
| **THURSDAY** | | | | |
| **FRIDAY** | | | | |

# Eastview High School: High Expectations

Located in a suburb of the Twin Cities next to 200 acres of playing fields and recreational facilities, Eastview High School is one of four high schools in a district serving 28,000 students.

At Eastview, students pursue and succeed with very rigorous coursework:

- In 2005, 86% of the Eastview students who took AP tests achieved a score of 3 or higher.

- Eastview surpasses the state and the district on the Minnesota Comprehensive Assessments, scoring 96 in 10th-grade reading (versus the state average of 81) and 91 in 11th-grade math (versus the state average of 74).

Eastview students are well-rounded in athletics and the arts as well, thanks to the dedication of Eastview's teachers: 90% coach or advise a cocurricular activity. In 2005, Eastview was named a "National Speech and Debate Combined School of Excellence." Only four schools in the nation received this annual award. Eastview won two of six categories at the National Forensic League National Speech Tournament and was the only school in the nation with two national champions.

> *Eastview High School, in Apple Valley, Minnesota, has used PLC concepts to earn the state's highest rating (10 stars) in multiple years for routinely producing top test scores.* Newsweek *has cited Eastview as one of America's best high schools each time the magazine has presented its report this decade. The school stands as a tribute to the dedication of its staff and the power of professional learning communities.*
> —Richard Dewey, Principal

| | | | | |
|---|---|---|---|---|
| **MONDAY** | | | | |
| **TUESDAY** | | | | |
| **WEDNESDAY** | | | | |
| **THURSDAY** | | | | |
| **FRIDAY** | | | | |

# A Culture of Celebration

*While recovering from chemotherapy, I was sitting on the couch feeling pretty depressed. Suddenly, a police car drove up with lights flashing. I met the officer at the door—I just knew that something terrible had happened at school.*

*The officer scooped me up and put me in his car. As we drove through town, police cars were everywhere. "What is going on?" I asked.*

*The officer replied, "Clara, you celebrate everything. It's now time we celebrate you. It's time for you to get back to work. . . . We need you."*

*I walked into the gym, and there were my students, all 648 of them. It was one of the most memorable moments of my life. The choir sang "Hero" and "Lean On Me," the band played, and the students rolled out a huge plastic banner that read, "WHATEVER IT TAKES." Then the student council president read her speech:*

*"Mrs. Davis, we just wanted to let you know that we have missed you very much, and things are not the same here without you. We need you to do 'whatever it takes' to get back home, and we'll do 'whatever it takes' to make sure that Freeport remains the place where great things happen. You are always there to support us when we need you, so let us return the favor. We love you. You can 'Lean On Us.'"*

*When kids embrace a culture committed to doing whatever it takes to help others realize their dreams, PLCs take on a whole new level.*

—Clara Sale-Davis, Principal,
Freeport Intermediate School, Freeport, TX

| MONDAY | | | | |
| --- | --- | --- | --- | --- |
| TUESDAY | | | | |
| WEDNESDAY | | | | |
| THURSDAY | | | | |
| FRIDAY | | | | |

*Professional Learning Communities at Work Plan Book*

Week Beginning:_____

# Why Teach?

*If you believe it is important to help children
and young men and women
acquire the knowledge, skills, and dispositions
essential to productive and satisfying lives,
then consider being a teacher.*

*If you are committed to your own lifelong learning,
to an ongoing study of the art and science of your craft,
then consider being a teacher.*

*If you truly enjoy kids, if you are able to see the best in
each of them,
if you are willing to persist
when confronted by their recalcitrance or indifference,
then consider being a teacher.*

*If you feel joy in seeing students learn to believe in
themselves
because you helped them achieve what they felt was
beyond their grasp,
then consider being a teacher.*

*If, like Henry Adams, you understand that, as a teacher,
you can affect eternity because it is impossible to tell
where your influence stops,
then consider being a teacher.*

*If you recognize that giving of yourself to others and
developing others
can be one of the most significant and fulfilling ways
in which to live your life,
then consider being a teacher.*

Used with permission of the National Staff Development Council, www.nsdc.org, 2006. All rights reserved.

# References and Resources

## References

Barth, R. (1991). Restructuring schools: Some questions for teachers and principals. *Phi Delta Kappan, 73*(2), 123–128.

DuFour, R. (2000). Why teach? *Journal of Staff Development, 21*(3). Available at www.nsdc.org/library/publications/gsd/dufour213.cfm.

Ferriter, B. (2005). The day I was very wrong: A lesson in professional learning communities. *Journal of Staff Development, 26*(3), 60, 72.

Marzano, R. (2003). *What works in schools: Translating research into action.* Alexandria, VA: ASCD.

O'Neill, J., & Conzemius, A. (2006). *The power of SMART goals: Using goals to improve student learning.* Bloomington, IN: Solution Tree.

Perkins, D. (2003). *King Arthur's roundtable.* New York: Wiley.

Reeves, D. (2002). *The leader's guide to standards: A blueprint for educational equity and excellence.* San Francisco: John Wiley and Sons.

## Resources

DuFour, R., DuFour, R., Eaker, R., & Karhanek, G. (2004). *Whatever it takes: How professional learning communities respond when kids don't learn.* Bloomington, IN: Solution Tree (formerly National Educational Service).

DuFour, R., DuFour, R., Eaker, R., & Many, T. (2006). *Learning by doing: A handbook for professional learning communities at work.* Bloomington, IN: Solution Tree (formerly National Educational Service).

DuFour, R., & Eaker, R. (1998). *Professional learning communities at work: Best practices for enhancing student achievement.* Bloomington, IN: Solution Tree (formerly National Educational Service).

DuFour, R., Eaker, R., & DuFour, R. (Eds.) (2005). *On common ground: The power of professional learning communities.* Bloomington, IN: Solution Tree (formerly National Educational Service).

Eaker, R., DuFour, R., & DuFour, R. (2002). *Getting started: Reculturing schools to become professional learning communities.* Bloomington, IN: Solution Tree (formerly National Educational Service).

## Make the Most of Your Professional Development Investment

Let Solution Tree (formerly National Educational Service) schedule time for you and your staff with leading practitioners in the areas of:

- Professional Learning Communities with Richard DuFour, Robert Eaker, Rebecca DuFour, and associates

- Effective Schools with associates of Larry Lezotte

- Assessment *for* Learning with Rick Stiggins and associates

- Crisis Management and Response with Cheri Lovre

- Classroom Management with Lee Canter and associates

- Discipline With Dignity with Richard Curwin and Allen Mendler

- PASSport to Success (parental involvement) with Vickie Burt

- Peacemakers (violence prevention) with Jeremy Shapiro

Additional presentations are available in the following areas:

- At-Risk Youth Issues

- Bullying Prevention/Teasing and Harassment

- Team Building and Collaborative Teams

- Data Collection and Analysis

- Embracing Diversity

- Literacy Development

- Motivating Techniques for Staff and Students

**Solution Tree**

304 West Kirkwood Avenue
Bloomington, IN 47404-5131
(812) 336-7700
(800) 733-6786 (toll free)
FAX (812) 336-7790
email: info@solution-tree.com
www.solution-tree.com

## NEED MORE COPIES OR ADDITIONAL RESOURCES ON THIS TOPIC?

Need more copies of this book? Want your own copy? Need additional resources on this topic? If so, you can order additional materials by using this form or by calling us toll free at (800) 733-6786 or (812) 336-7700. Or you can order by FAX at (812) 336-7790 or visit our website at www.solution-tree.com.

| Title | Price* | Quantity | Total |
|---|---|---|---|
| Professional Learning Communities at Work Plan Book | $12.95 | | |
| Getting Started | 19.95 | | |
| Learning by Doing (includes CD-ROM) | 27.95 | | |
| On Common Ground | 29.95 | | |
| Professional Learning Communities at Work | 24.95 | | |
| Professional Learning Communities at Work (video set) | 495.00 | | |
| Professional Learning Communities at Work (online course) | 349.00 | | |
| Through New Eyes (video) | 174.95 | | |
| Whatever It Takes (audio book) | 27.95 | | |
| The Handbook for SMART School Teams | 54.95 | | |
| | | SUBTOTAL | |
| | | SHIPPING | |
| Continental U.S.: Please add 6% of order total. | | | |
| Outside continental U.S.: Please add 8% of order total. | | | |
| | | HANDLING | |
| Continental U.S.: Please add $4. Outside continental U.S.: Please add $6. | | | |
| | | TOTAL (U.S. funds) | |

*Price subject to change without notice.

❏ Check enclosed    ❏ Purchase order enclosed
❏ Money order        ❏ VISA, MasterCard, Discover, or American Express (circle one)

Credit Card No._____ Exp. Date _____

Cardholder Signature _____

**SHIP TO:**

First Name_____ Last Name _____

Position_____

Institution Name _____

Address _____

City_____ State_____ ZIP _____

Phone_____ FAX _____

Email_____

**Solution Tree**

Solution Tree (formerly National Educational Service)
304 West Kirkwood Avenue • Bloomington, IN 47404-5131
(812) 336-7700 • (800) 733-6786 (toll free) • FAX (812) 336-7790
email: orders@solution-tree.com • www.solution-tree.com